SUGAR GROVE PUBLIC LIBRARY DISTRICT
54 Snow Street/P.O. Box 1049
Sugar Grove, IL 60554
(630) 466-4686

W9-BPP-483

THE WORLD
OF THE CELL
LIFE ON A SMALL SCALE

Robert Snedden

Series Editor Andrew
Solway

Heinemann Library
Chicago, Illinois

Customer Service 888-454-2279

Visit our website at www.heinemannlibrary.com

Designed by Paul Davies and Associates
Illustrations by Wooden Ark
Originated by Ambassador Litho Ltd
Printed by Wing King Tong in Hong Kong

07 06 05 04 03
10 9 8 7 6 5 4 3 2 1

Library of Congress Cataloging-in-Publication Data
Snedden, Robert.
  The world of the cell : life on a small scale / Robert Snedden.
       v. cm. -- (Cells and life)
Includes index.
Contents: All life is cells -- Cell shapes and sizes -- Looking at cells
-- The electron microscope -- Cell structure -- Proteins and DNA --
Cells and energy -- Releasing energy -- Aerobic respiration -- Bacteria:
the prokaryotes -- Bacterial metabolism -- Bacterial behavior --
Viruses -- The eukaryotes -- Inside the cytoplasm -- Plant and animal
cells -- Protistans -- Protozoans -- First cells -- Building cells.
  ISBN 1-58810-676-4 (HC) 1-58810-938-0 (Pbk.)
 1. Cells--Juvenile literature. [1. Cells.] I. Title. II. Series.
  QH582.5 .S65 2002
  571.6--dc21
                                    2001008592

Acknowledgments
The author and publishers are grateful to the following for permission to reproduce copyright material:
pp. 5, 42 A. Pasieka/Science Photo Library; pp. 7, 16, 35 J. Burgess/Science Photo Library; p. 9 S. Cinti,
Universite D'ancon, CNRI/Science Photo Library; p. 12 G. Murti/Science Photo Library; p. 14 M. F.
Chillmaid/Science Photo Library; pp. 15, 28 Eye of Science/Science Photo Library; pp. 19, 32 M .
Abbey/Science Photo Library; p. 20 B. Longcore/Science Photo Library; p. 24 E. Grave/Science Photo
Library; p. 25 M. Kage/Science Photo Library; pp. 26, 39(top), 39(bottom) A. Syred/Science Photo
Library; p. 27 K. H. Kjeldsen/Science Photo Library; p.30 J. King-Holmes/Science Photo Library; p. 31
Photodisc; p. 33 K. Lounatmaa/Science Photo Library; p. 34 L. Itannard, UCT/Science Photo Library; p.
37 Biozentrum, University of Basel/Science Photo Library; p. 37 D. Patterson /Science Photo Library; p.
41 R White/Corbis; p. 43 M. Rohde, gbf/Science Photo Library.

Cover photograph reproduced with permission of Science Photo Library/Astrid and Hans-Frieder Michler.

Every effort has been made to contact copyright holders of any material reproduced in this book.
Any omissions will be rectified in subsequent printings if notice is given to the publisher.

Our thanks to Richard Fosbery for his comments in the preparation of this book.

Some words are shown in bold, **like this.** You can find out what they mean
by looking in the glossary.

Contents

1 All Life Is Cells

Living cells are amazing things. A single cell is too small for us to see without the help of a **microscope,** and yet this tiny package of chemicals has all the properties of life. Cells are the smallest units of life. They are life's building blocks. The simplest forms of life, such as bacteria, are single cells. The more complex plants and animals we see around us, including humans, are built from great assemblies of cells, millions upon millions of them all working together. In fact, there are more than 10 trillion cells in the human body.

A cell is not a simple unchanging structure. It is a living, dynamic thing that carries out many different jobs. Cells can grow and reproduce, they respond to changes in their environment, and they adapt to changing conditions.

Cell theory

Cell theory grew from studies of the cell carried out by scientists in the 1800s. Its three points still hold true today.

1. Every **organism** is composed of one or more cells.
2. The cell is the smallest unit that has the properties of life.
3. All life arises from the growth and division of single cells.

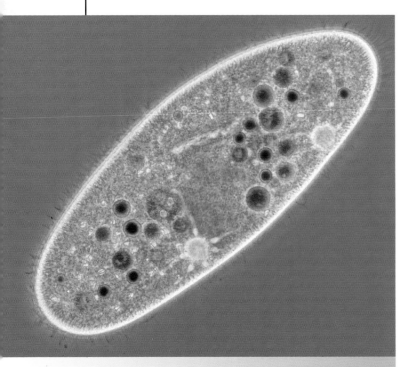

The simplest forms of life are single cells. *Paramecium* is a single-celled creature that is part of a group called **protistans.** It feeds on other protistans. Magnification approx. x 1,000.

Recipe for a cell

At one time cells were thought to be little more than tiny droplets of living material, called protoplasm. We now know that they are a little more complex than that. All cells have a thin outer membrane. Plant cells have a tough cell wall as well as a membrane. Within this outer skin is an incredibly complex "soup" of water and many different substances. Vast numbers of chemical reactions are going on in this soup all the time, as substances are arranged and rearranged, broken apart, and joined together again in different ways. Between 70 and 80 percent of a cell's weight is water.

Cells are made from several basic ingredients that are essential to all life. All of them are large **molecules** made from chains of smaller repeating units.

Proteins are part of many cell structures, including the membrane, and proteins called **enzymes** control the many chemical reactions in the cell. **Lipids** (fats) are the other main substance in membranes, and they also store energy. **Carbohydrates** are made from long chains of sugars. They are the cell's main source of energy. **Nucleic acids** such as **deoxyribonucleic acid (DNA)** are the cell's genetic material. DNA contains information the cell needs to grow and reproduce.

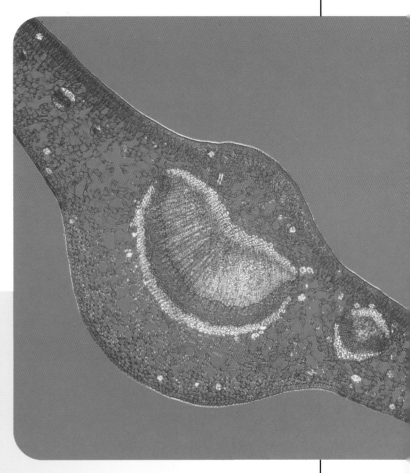

This is a cross section of a leaf from an evergreen shrub, as seen through a light microscope. The image shows the leaf is made up of thousands of cells. The pinkish areas are the leaf's veins. The cells here are specialized to carry water and nutrients around the plant. Magnification approx. x 40.

Little rooms

In 1665 Robert Hooke, a scientist working in London, used a microscope that he had built himself to examine thin slices of cork (cork is made from the bark of trees). Hooke's microscope could only magnify objects about 30 times. But this was enough to show a honeycomb-like network of tiny, boxlike compartments in the cork. Hooke called these little compartments cellulae, from a Latin word meaning "little rooms." From this we get our word *cells*.

What Hooke saw in the cork were the empty cell walls of dead plant tissue. He had noticed that cells in living plants were filled with what he called "juices," but his microscope was not powerful enough to show any details of the inside of the cell.

Cell Shapes and Sizes

How small is a cell? Many are very small indeed. To measure cells using everyday units would be hopeless, as most cells are about 1/1,000 of an inch (0.0025 centimeter) in diameter. Bacterial cells are among the smallest of all cells. In fact, some bacterial cells are so small that if you lined 50,000 of them in a row, they would measure only 1 inch (2.5 centimeters).

A few types of cells are big enough to be seen with the naked eye. The inside of a bird's egg, for example, is really a single cell. Some nerve cells, such as those in a giraffe's neck, can be more than three feet long.

But why are most cells so small? Why don't living things have a few big cells, instead of millions of small ones?

Surface and volume

Cells stay so small because of surface area to volume ratio. Think of a simple cell as being a cube measuring 10 in. (25 cm) on each side. The volume of the cell is 10 x 10 x 10 = 1,000 in³, and its surface area is 10 x 10 x 6 = 600 in².

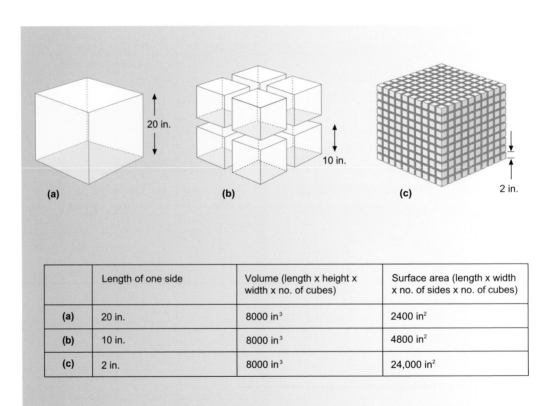

	Length of one side	Volume (length x height x width x no. of cubes)	Surface area (length x width x no. of sides x no. of cubes)
(a)	20 in.	8000 in³	2400 in²
(b)	10 in.	8000 in³	4800 in²
(c)	2 in.	8000 in³	24,000 in²

In this diagram, the single cube, the eight smaller cubes, and the 1,000 very small cubes all have the same total volume: 8,000 cubic inches. However, the surface area of the 1,000 small cubes is 10 times greater than that of the single cube.

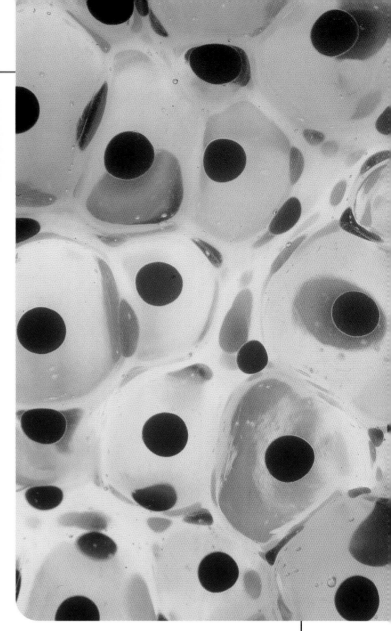

Each egg in this frog spawn was initially a single cell. The cell divides many times as it grows. Magnification approx. x 8.

If you double the length of each side to 20 in. (50 cm), then the cell's volume becomes 20 x 20 x 20 = 8,000 in.^{3}, which is not twice but eight times greater than the original volume. However, the surface area becomes 20 x 20 x 6 = 2,400 in.^{2}, which is only four times greater. This means that each part of the cell's surface has to transport nutrients and waste in and out of the cell for twice as much of the inside as it did before. The bigger the cell becomes, the more its surface area lags behind its volume. If the cell becomes too big, it becomes impossible for it to get nutrients in and waste out fast enough.

Once inside the cell, nutrients have to get to the places where they are needed. In the small-scale world of the cell, there are no veins or arteries to transport materials. Instead, the cell relies on the **diffusion** of **molecules** through its interior. Such a transport system simply does not work once the cell grows beyond a certain size.

For a chemical reaction to take place in a cell (or anywhere else for that matter), the chemicals reacting together must come into contact with each other. If a cell doubled in size, it would have to manufacture eight times more chemicals to ensure that reactions took place.

So how is it possible for cells to grow to three feet in length? Well, egg cells can be large because most of the cell is yolk. The yolk is a stored food supply for the growing embryo, which does not need food from any other source. Other big cells are either long and thin or have many folds and indentations. These shapes help to increase the cell's surface area.

Cell Structure

Cells come in a variety of sizes and shapes and carry out a range of activities. Yet they have features in common. All cells have an outer skin, the **cell membrane.** Within this membrane, the cell can be divided into two areas: an area containing the cell's genetic material **(DNA)** and the **cytoplasm,** which contains everything else the cell needs to carry out its functions.

Prokaryotes and eukaryotes

At the most basic level, cells can be divided into two types. In one type, the cell's genetic material is surrounded by a membrane, forming a structure called the **nucleus.** Such cells are known as **eukaryotes** (meaning "true nucleus"). In the other, simpler cell type, the genetic material is not enclosed by a membrane. Such cells are called **prokaryotes** (meaning "before nucleus"). Bacteria are prokaryotes, while all other cells, including the cells that make up all plants and animals, are eukaryotes. Eukaryotes are generally bigger than prokaryotes.

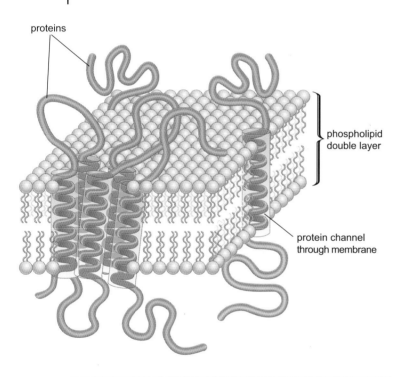

proteins

phospholipid double layer

protein channel through membrane

A cell membrane is a double layer of phospholipid molecules (fats with a phosphate group on one end). The tails of the lipid molecules repel water and face toward the middle of the membrane. Proteins embedded in the membrane act as pathways that allow certain molecules to pass through.

Cell walls and membranes

The cell membrane, or **plasma membrane,** is the boundary between the cell and the rest of the world. A cell cannot be completely isolated from its environment, because it needs to take in raw materials from outside the cell and get rid of the waste products it produces. The cell membrane controls what can come into the cell from outside and what can leave it.

Some cells, notably those of plants and bacteria, also have a tough external cell wall outside the cell membrane. In plants, this wall is made of **cellulose.** It surrounds the cell and provides protection and strength. Bacteria may have a third layer of protection, a slimy material called the slime capsule.

A cell membrane is selectively, or partially, permeable. This means that some substances can get in and out, but others cannot. The membrane is made up of a double sheet of **lipid,** with **proteins** embedded in the surface. Some of these proteins provide channels through which some substances can pass in and out of the cell. Other proteins act as pumps, actively moving substances in and out of the cell.

In animals, objects that are too large to pass through the cell membrane can get into the cell by a process called **endocytosis.** The membrane folds around the object to form a small bubble, called a **vesicle,** which passes into the cell.

The nucleus

The nucleus is the central, somewhat round area in eukaryote cells where the genetic material is found. It is surrounded by a double membrane, called the nuclear envelope. Pores (small holes) in the envelope control the passage of **molecules** in and out of the nucleus. The nucleus contains a complete set of the **organism's** genes. The genes contain instructions for making proteins. Proteins control the way the cell develops and functions.

Cytoplasm

The cytoplasm includes everything found between the cell membrane and the nuclear membrane. In eukaryotes, the cytoplasm contains many different structures, called **organelles.** Each organelle has a specific job within the cell.

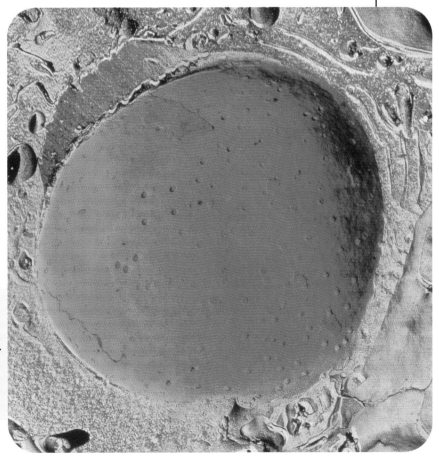

A close-up of a cell's nuclear membrane (or envelope) shows the nuclear pores. Magnification approx. x 15,000.

2 Inside a Eukaryote Cell

Eukaryote cells have a more complicated structure than the simple **prokaryotes.** The inside of a eukaryote contains many different structures called **organelles.** Each organelle has a specialized function. Organelles called **mitochondria,** for example, store most of the **enzymes** and other chemicals that the cell needs to get energy from food.

Organelles separate the different chemical reactions within the cell. Each organelle can bring together and store the various materials it needs to carry out these reactions. Packaging the chemicals for particular processes in this way allows the cell to operate much more efficiently.

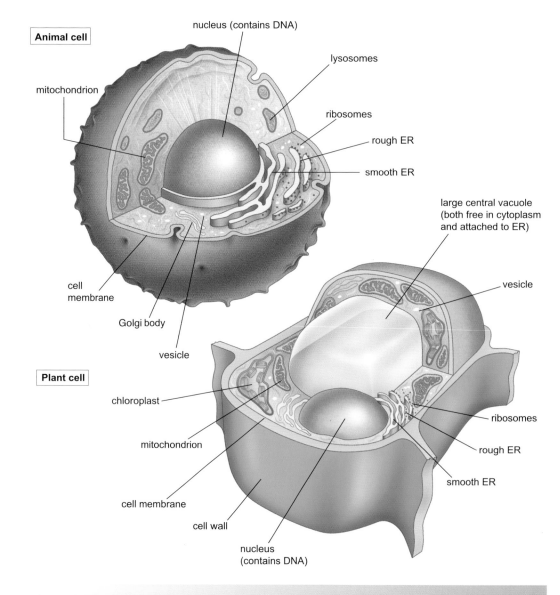

Shown here are cutaway views of a typical plant cell and a typical animal cell. Both plant and animal cells are eukaryotes. Unlike animal cells, plant cells have a rigid cell wall and a large sap-filled cavity (the **vacuole**) that fills most of the cell.

A typical cell

Although a typical animal cell and a typical plant cell are shown on the opposite page, in reality there is no such thing as a typical cell, any more than there is a typical plant or a typical animal. All cells have the same basic plan, but there are hundreds of variations on the theme. The common features of eukaryote cells are listed in the table below.

Common features of the eukaryote cell	
Nucleus	Contains the cell's genetic material, or **DNA**.
Mitochondria	The cell's powerhouses, where energy from food is made available.
Chloroplasts	Organelles found only in plant cells. **Chloroplasts** are where **photosynthesis** takes place. This is the process by which plants make food from sunlight, water, and carbon dioxide from the air.
Ribosome	Tiny, roundish structures where small **molecules** called **amino acids** are joined together to make **proteins**.
Endoplasmic reticulum	A network of membranes within the cell. Most of the cell's **ribosomes** are found on the **endoplasmic reticulum** (ER).
Golgi body	Organelles where the final stages of protein assembly are carried out. Proteins for use outside the cell are completed in the **Golgi body**.
Vesicles	Small membrane sacs that perform a variety of functions, including breaking down (digesting) substances absorbed by the cell.
Tubules and filaments	Tiny tubes and fibers that form a "cell skeleton." The tubules and fibers can contract (shorten). They are important for movement of the whole cell and for cell division.

Within the Cytoplasm

As mentioned earlier, the **cytoplasm** is all the parts of a cell between the **cell membrane** and the **nucleus.** All the cell's internal membranes and **organelles,** such as the **mitochondria** and **chloroplasts,** are suspended in a jellylike material called **cytosol.** In many cells the cytosol and organelles are organized by a microscopic network of **protein** filaments called the **cytoskeleton.**

The cell skeleton

Every cell has a cytoskeleton, which gives it shape and controls its movement. It is made up of two types of structures: **microtubules** and **microfilaments.**

Microtubules are rigid, hollow protein tubes. They are found throughout the cytoplasm, either singly or in bundles. Microtubules can be quickly put together or taken apart when the cell needs them. A cell structure attached to one end of a microtubule can be pushed or pulled through the **cytoplasm** by lengthening or shortening the microtubule. It is similar to pushing a boat into the water by pushing against the bank with a pole. Plant cells can move chloroplasts around in this way, arranging them in the best positions to absorb sunlight.

Microfilaments are made of a different type of protein. They are solid and much thinner than microtubules. A weblike network of microfilaments is attached to the membrane and helps give shape to the cell. Microfilaments are also involved in cell movement. Some single-celled **organisms** move about by extending temporary pseudopods (meaning "false feet"). Inside each pseudopod, hundreds of microfilaments grow rapidly in length, dragging the cell membrane along with them.

This magnified photo of cells shows the cytoskeleton. The bluish ovals are cell nuclei. The microtubules are stained red. The microfilaments are green. Magnification approx. x 3,500.

Protein production lines

The **endoplasmic reticulum** (ER) and the **Golgi bodies** form a network of membranes within the cell called the **cytomembrane system.** This is where large **molecules,** in particular **lipids** and proteins, are put together.

The ER runs throughout the cytoplasm. In animal cells it is a continuation of the nuclear membrane. There are two types, rough ER and smooth ER. The outside of the rough ER is covered with tiny **ribosomes.** The ribosomes are where protein molecules are made. Ribosomes are also found on the nuclear membrane and scattered through the cytoplasm.

The ribosomes on the rough ER make proteins that are destined for use outside the cell. Many cells produce proteins for use elsewhere. For example, the cells of your pancreas (part of your digestive system) produce **enzymes** that help to digest food. These cells have a lot of rough ER.

Smooth ER has no ribosomes and is less common than rough ER. It curves through the cytoplasm like a series of interconnected pipes. It plays a part in assembling different parts of the cell membrane.

Golgi bodies consist of a stack of folded membranes similar to a pile of flattened pancakes. If the rough ER is a protein production line, then the Golgi body is the dispatcher, "addressing" the proteins to make sure they reach the right destinations and then sending them out.

Many of the proteins will already have been labeled by the rough ER, but they may be relabeled as they pass through the Golgi body. This final sorting process is important, as it allows the proteins to link up with specific target molecules later on. The proteins are then packaged up in **vesicles** once more and sent off to their final destinations.

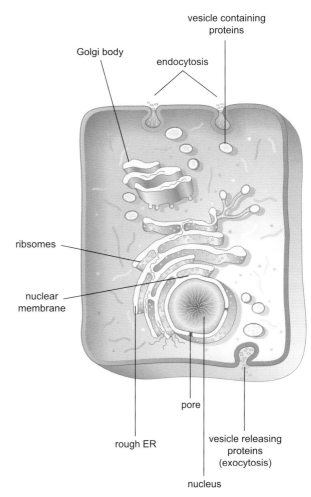

Golgi body

endocytosis

vesicle containing proteins

ribsomes

nuclear membrane

pore

rough ER

vesicle releasing proteins (exocytosis)

nucleus

This diagram shows the cell's cytomembrane system. Proteins are assembled in the endoplasmic reticulum (ER). They then move to the Golgi body in vesicles for final changes.

Plant and Animal Cells

Plant and animal cells have some important differences. One of the most obvious differences is the plant cell wall, the rigid outer covering surrounding the **cell membrane.** The cell wall is made of fibers of **cellulose,** a type of **carbohydrate.** The rigidity of a plant cell wall places a limit on how far the cell can expand and grow.

Cellulose and nutrition

Although herbivores such as cows and sheep eat plants, they cannot actually produce the enzymes needed to break down cellulose into sugars. Instead, they have to rely on colonies of bacteria living inside their guts, which do have the ability to produce this enzyme. Without their bacterial helpers, herbivores would not get the nutrition they need.

Plant cells also have **chloroplasts,** which animal cells do not have. Chloroplasts are the cell **organelles** where the process of **photosynthesis** takes place. They are only found in the parts of plants that are exposed to light. Many single-celled **organisms** also have chloroplasts.

Vacuoles

Vacuoles are found in both plant and animal cells, but only plant cells have a large central vacuole. This large, membrane-bound space contains a solution of sugars and salts called sap. The central vacuole takes up most of the space in a mature plant cell. The **cytoplasm** and **nucleus** are squeezed into a thin layer between it and the cell wall.

The castor oil plant (*Fatsia japonica*) on the left is healthy and turgid. The one on the right has lost water and has consequently wilted. It is no longer healthy and cannot support itself.

The sap inside the vacuole is a more concentrated solution of chemicals than in the rest of the cell, so water tends to move into the vacuole (a process called **osmosis**). This causes the vacuole to expand and push the cell contents up against the inside of the cell wall. The cell then becomes turgid (firm and plump). When a plant has enough water, all its cells are turgid, and this keeps the plant upright. If fluid is lost from the vacuole, the cell collapses. You can see this happening when a plant in need of water wilts.

Cilia and flagella

Some animal cells have slender, mobile structures called **cilia** and **flagella.** They stick out from the cell membrane and are used for movement. Plant cells do not have cilia or flagella.

Flagella are long, whiplike structures that tend to occur singly. The tails of sperm cells are flagella. Cilia are found in large numbers and look a lot like hair. They beat together like the oars on a boat. Some single-celled organisms are covered in a layer of tiny cilia that move them through their watery environment. Cilia are also found in various parts of the human body. For example, the cells that line the airways of the lungs are covered in cilia.

Lysosomes

Lysosomes are sometimes found in plant cells but are more often found in animal cells. These spherical bodies are separated from the rest of the cell by membranes and contain powerful digestive **enzymes.** Their function is to destroy worn-out organelles or to digest food particles absorbed into the cell. The digested food is then passed back through the membrane to be used by the cell.

If lysosomes break, the enzymes released into the cytoplasm digest and kill the cell. This happens when dead tissue rots and is one reason why food spoils. Lysosome enzymes are also involved in the development of a tadpole into an adult frog. As the tadpole matures, its tail slowly disappears. This happens because lysosome enzymes are released to destroy the unwanted cells of the tail.

This photo taken with a scanning **electron microscope,** shows the cilia that line the air passages of the lungs. A layer of mucus traps dirt and other particles, which the cilia then sweep out of the lungs. Magnification approx. x 6,000.

Light for life

All cells need organic, carbon-containing compounds for growth and repair. At the same time cells need a source of energy to carry out all this activity. Living things get organic compounds and energy mainly through **photosynthesis.** In photosynthesis, plants take the simple **molecules** carbon dioxide (from the atmosphere) and water (from the ground). Then they use the energy of sunlight to build these molecules into more complex organic compounds that provide food, not only for the plant but also for other living things. All animals rely on plants as their food source, or on other animals that have eaten plants. Without plants, the earth would not be able to sustain the rich variety of life around us.

Catching the light

Most plants are green. But why? The colors of a plant come from the pigments within its cells. Pigments are molecules that absorb light. And the color of a pigment depends on which wavelengths of light it absorbs and which it reflects. There are many pigments in the living world. But in plants, the most important of them is a green pigment called **chlorophyll.** This pigment gives green plants their color.

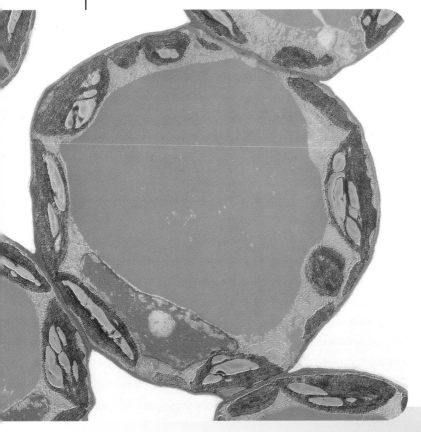

Most of the chlorophyll in plant cells is found in large **organelles** called **chloroplasts.** Photosynthesis occurs in the chloroplasts. Chlorophyll plays a crucial role in this process. First, chlorophyll molecules, helped by other pigments, trap light energy from the sun. This energy is used to start a chain of reactions that split water molecules into hydrogen and oxygen. This process releases chemical energy. The plant is able to capture this energy and store it in the bonds of a molecule called **adenosine triphosphate (ATP).**

These chloroplasts in a plant leaf cell are color enhanced. The chloroplasts are the pink and green oval-shaped structures around the large blue **vacuole** in the center of the cell. The pink areas in the chloroplasts are starch grains. Magnification approx. x 4,500.

Capturing carbon

Once plant cells have captured energy from sunlight, they can use it to build new molecules. This process begins when carbon dioxide molecules drift into the air spaces in a leaf. Eventually they come upon a photosynthetic cell. Passing into the cell, the molecules reach a chloroplast. Here, an **enzyme** called rubisco grabs hold of the carbon dioxide and attaches it to another carbon compound. This is called carbon fixation, and it is the the first step in the process that will result in the production of sugars such as **glucose.** These sugars are the building blocks of **carbohydrates** such as **cellulose** and **starch.**

Essential waste

One product of the first stage in photosynthesis is oxygen, which is formed by the splitting of water. This waste product is as important to animals as sugar and the other foods they get from plants. This is because almost all living things need oxygen for **aerobic respiration,** which is the most efficient way of getting energy from food.

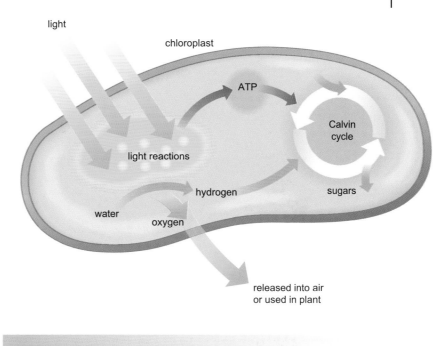

light

chloroplast

ATP

Calvin cycle

light reactions

hydrogen

sugars

water

oxygen

released into air or used in plant

During the light reaction stage of photosynthesis, light energy is used to split water and energy is transferred to the chemical bonds of ATP. Hydrogen from the splitting of water and energy from ATP are used to convert carbon dioxide into sugars.

Autumn accessories

Among the other pigments in green plants are the **carotenoids.** These pigments are red, orange, and yellow in color. In most plants their color is masked by the large quantities of chlorophyll. However, in the autumn, they become visible in the leaves of deciduous trees (trees that lose their leaves) when the chlorophyll in the leaves is broken down.

Releasing Energy

Living things need energy for all of the things they do. Plants can tap into the vast source of energy from the sun and use it to make **ATP,** the chemical energy of life. Plants then store this energy in energy-rich **molecules** such as **glucose.** Other living things get their energy by eating food—either plants or creatures that have eaten plants. This food contains glucose and other chemicals, which can be broken down to release chemical energy. This energy is used to make ATP.

The process by which cells break down food molecules to release energy in the form of ATP is called **respiration.** In most **organisms** this process requires oxygen and is called **aerobic respiration.** Some cells (many bacteria, for example) are anaerobic, which means they can get energy from food without using oxygen.

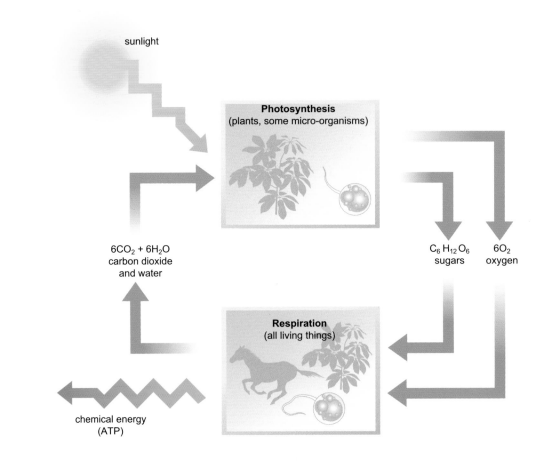

This diagram shows the connection between **photosynthesis** and aerobic respiration. The end product of photosynthesis is oxygen and energy in the form of sugar. Respiration uses the oxygen to release energy from sugar, producing carbon dioxide and water. Carbon dioxide and water are the raw materials for photosynthesis.

Glycolysis

Whether a cell obtains its energy by aerobic or **anaerobic respiration,** the process begins in the same way. In the **cytoplasm** of the cell, **enzymes** split glucose molecules in a process called **glycolysis.** The initial steps of this reaction actually require energy and use up two ATP molecules. However, in the course of the reaction four new ATP molecules are formed. Therefore, there is a net gain of two ATP per glucose molecule.

Anaerobic respiration

A wide variety of living things use anaerobic respiration. Examples are bacteria and other single-celled organisms that live in places where there is little oxygen, such as marshes, stagnant ponds, and inside the guts of animals. The bacteria used to make yogurt and the yeasts used to make bread all use anaerobic respiration.

Organisms that use anaerobic respiration get energy from glycolysis, but then go a step further to form end products. One such end product, lactate, is sometimes referred to as **lactic acid.** The bacteria that produce cheese and yogurt use anaerobic respiration in this way. Lactate is also formed in muscle cells when they have to produce energy quickly.

Another kind of anaerobic respiration has ethanol (alcohol) as the end product. Yeasts, which we use to make bread, brew beer, and make wine, use this pathway. Wild yeast cells live on grapes and other fruits and berries. Birds sometimes get drunk by feasting on naturally **fermenting** berries!

A photograph taken with a light **microscope** shows brewer's yeast, *Saccharomyces cerevisiae*. In the absence of oxygen, yeasts get energy by fermentation, converting sugars to ethanol (alcohol). Magnification approx. x 2,000.

Powerhouses of the Cell

Most cells obtain their energy by **aerobic respiration.** This process requires oxygen and breaks down sugars to carbon dioxide and water.

If oxygen is available, aerobic respiration can occur. The products of **glycolysis** pass out of the **cytoplasm** and into the **mitochondria.** These rodlike or spherical **organelles** are often called the powerhouses of the cell. All cells except bacteria have them in their cytoplasm. They are a vital part of living cells, supplying most of their energy needs. The more active a cell is, the more mitochondria it has. Some cells, such as human liver cells, contain more than 1,000 mitochondria.

Inside the mitochondria, the products of glycolysis combine with oxygen and break down into water and carbon dioxide. The process involves a complex chain of chemical reactions called the **Krebs cycle,** or the citric acid cycle, and releases large amounts of energy. Aerobic respiration is much more efficient than **anaerobic respiration.** Overall, 32 **ATP molecules** are produced from a single molecule of **glucose,** 16 times more than the 2 ATP molecules produced by glycolysis alone.

The mitochondrial membrane

The mitochondrion has a double membrane. The outer membrane is smooth, but the inner membrane has many folds called **cristae.** The cristae are lined with tiny structures that contain the **enzymes** that break down chemicals and generate ATP. In cells that have high energy needs, the mitochondria have more cristae and thus more enzyme-containing structures.

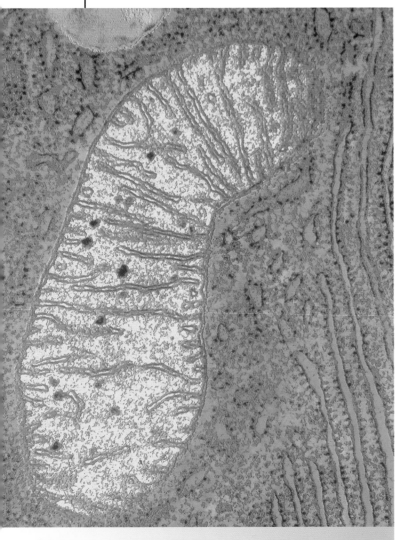

A false-color photograph taken with an **electron microscope** shows a mitochondrion. The membrane folds, or cristae, where respiration takes place can be seen within the mitochondrion. Magnification approx x 20,000.

Mitochondria and bacteria

Bacteria, unlike most other living cells, have no mitochondria. A typical bacterium, in fact, is very much like a free-living mitochondrion. Most scientists now believe that mitochondria evolved from bacteria. At a very early stage in the history of life, these bacteria began to live inside larger cells, eventually becoming a part of them.

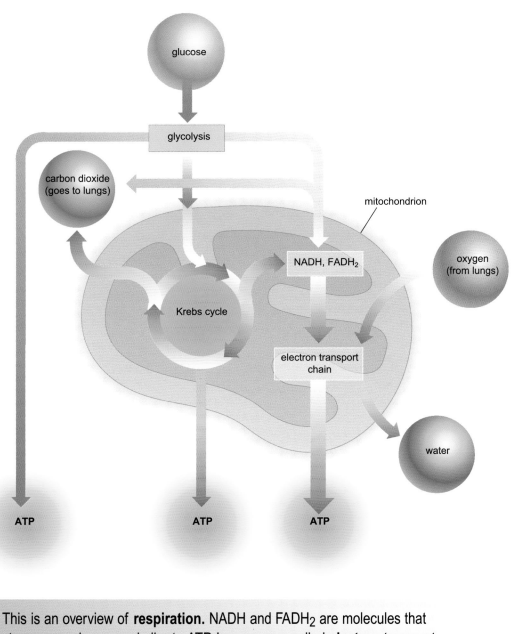

This is an overview of **respiration.** NADH and $FADH_2$ are molecules that store energy in a way similar to ATP. In a process called **electron** transport phosophorylation, the energy from NADH and $FADH_2$ is converted to ATP.

Protein Production

Probably the most complex and important of the large **molecules** in a cell are the **proteins.** All the structures of a cell are built mostly from proteins. A special class of proteins, called **enzymes,** controls the enormous range of chemical reactions that go on inside living cells.

Without enzymes there would be no life. A cell needs thousands of enzymes to perform its essential tasks, such as obtaining energy, moving, growing, and repairing itself. Each reaction that takes place in the cell has its own specific enzyme. Because the enzymes control the reactions, they effectively control the cell.

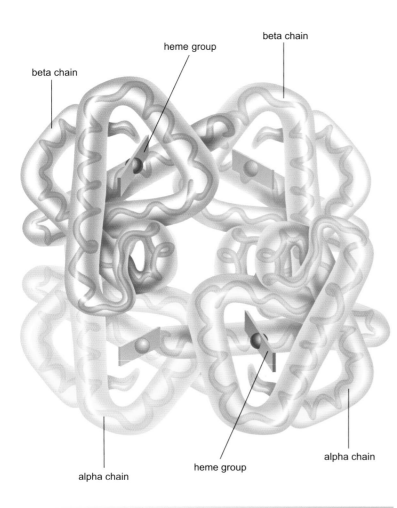

beta chain

heme group

beta chain

beta chain

alpha chain

heme group

alpha chain

Once a protein chain has formed, it may team up with other protein chains to form a complex protein. This illustration shows hemoglobin, a protein found in red blood cells. It is made up of four protein chains and four small molecules called heme groups.

Protein assembly

Proteins are complex, three-dimensional substances made of chains of smaller molecules called **amino acids.** There are twenty kinds of amino acid commonly used in protein building. Each protein has a very specific structure, with a certain number of amino acids in a particular order. So how does the cell ensure that the correct number of amino acids are linked in the right order to make a particular protein?

DNA

The instructions for assembling proteins in the cell are contained within the structure of another remarkable molecule—**deoxyribonucleic acid (DNA).** Like proteins, DNA molecules are made up of many smaller units. Each unit is one letter in a code that the cell can read. This code is called the genetic code, because it comes in segments called genes. Each gene is the template for building a protein or part of a protein.

Every living thing has a unique form of DNA. All forms of life, from the simplest single-celled bacterium to the most complex plants and animals, contain at least one DNA molecule. Whenever a cell divides, it first makes a copy of its DNA, so that each new cell has its own protein instruction kit.

Following the instructions

The **nucleus** is the largest and most conspicuous **organelle** in the cells of **eukaryotes.** This is where the cell's DNA is found. Bacteria have no nucleus, but they still have DNA in their **cytoplasm.** The DNA molecules are folded and coiled up to form structures called **chromosomes.** Just before a cell divides, the chromosomes coil even more and become visible.

In many cells, a dark, oval area called the **nucleolus** can be seen inside the nucleus. Here, parts of the chromosomes are unwound so that the protein assembly instructions can be read. Molecules of a substance called **messenger ribonucleic acid (mRNA),** which is similar to DNA, copy the instructions and carry them from the nucleus into the cytoplasm.

Messenger RNA goes to the **ribosomes,** where the proteins will be produced. A ribosome moves along the messenger RNA, following the instructions it carries. Amino acids are brought to the messenger RNA and linked together in the right order to form the protein.

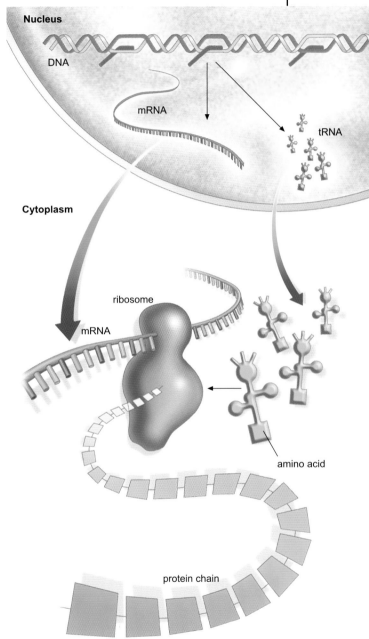

Shown here is an overview of protein synthesis. The instructions for making a protein are copied from DNA and carried from the nucleus to the cytoplasm by messenger RNA (mRNA). The mRNA goes to the ribosome, which reads the instructions and joins together amino acids in the order specified. Another molecule, transfer RNA (tRNA), is responsible for bringing amino acids to the ribosome.

3 Protistans

Protistans are difficult to classify. There are around 90,000 known living species, most of them single-celled **organisms.** They can be roughly divided into three main groups:

- funguslike protistans, such as water molds and slime molds
- animal-like protistans, known as the **protozoans** (meaning "first animals")
- plantlike protistans, which include the **algae.**

The protistans are **eukaryotes** and so can be readily distinguished from the other group of single-celled organisms, the bacteria. Unlike bacteria, protistans have a **nucleus** and **organelles** within their cells.

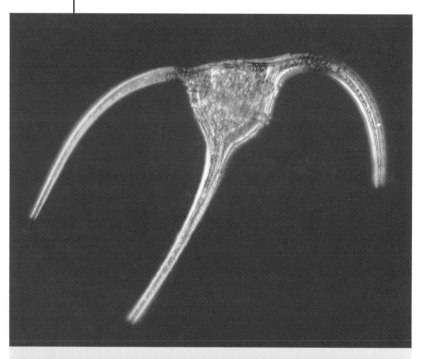

This is the dinoflagellate *Ceratium tripos*. Dinoflagellates are single-celled protistans, usually found in the ocean. They can either eat as animals do or photosynthesize as plants do. Magnification approx. x 1,250.

Protistans come in a variety of forms. Some have scales, shells, and highly elaborate skeletons. Some even form multicellular colonies. The colonies of some marine protistans are made up of hundreds of cells encased within a long tube more than three feet (1 meter) long. In contrast, some protistan **parasites** are small enough to invade the cells of other organisms.

Protistans are found practically everywhere. They have adapted to life across a range of habitats from polar oceans to tropical rain forests, and from the ocean floor to the summits of mountains. Even your body is a thriving habitat for protistans.

Plantlike protistans

Protistans capable of **photosynthesis** are often informally grouped together as members of the algae. This loose grouping also includes some multicellular organisms such as the red, green, and brown seaweeds. Some seaweeds are as big as trees. Most algae live in water, but a few live in damp places on land, such as on the surface of moist soil, damp rocks, and tree trunks. The majority are classed as **phytoplankton.** These are single-celled, water-living organisms that are the basic food of all animals in the oceans, rivers, and lakes.

- The green algae include about 7,000 species, ranging from *Chlorella* (a simple alga, made up of a single spherical cell containing one large **chloroplast**) to large seaweeds such as sea lettuce. Green algae are thought to be closely related to true plants because they have **cellulose** cell walls, use the same types of **chlorophyll,** and store food in the form of **starch.** The chlorophyll gives them a bright green color. Although **flagella** are characteristic of animal cells, some single-celled species of green alga are able to swim using flagella.

- The chrysophytes are mostly free-living photosynthesizers. The golden and yellow-green algae included in this group get their color from photosynthetic pigments called **carotenoids.** Most chrysophytes live in fresh water.

- Euglenoids are single-celled organisms that are difficult to classify as they have some animal and some plant characteristics. They can move around using a flagellum, a characteristic of animal cells. Most of them have chloroplasts, a characteristic of plant cells, but some do not. Unlike green algae, they do not store food as starch, and they lack rigid cellulose cell walls. They have a **protein** coat called a pellicle instead. There are about 1,000 species.

- Diatoms are common in marine and freshwater habitats. They have intricate, jewel-like shells formed from two perforated parts that overlap like the lid on a box.

- The 1,200 or so species of dinoflagellate typically have two **flagella** for getting around and an outer protective coat formed from plates of cellulose. This coat varies enormously in shape among species. Dinoflagellates live in both freshwater and seawater.

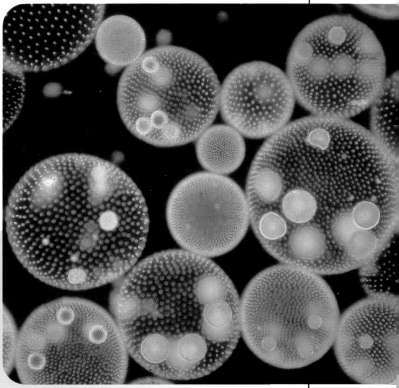

Colonies of the protistan *Volvox* whirl around. The individual *Volvox* cells each have a whiplike flagellum. Each colony is a hollow ball of between 500 and 10,000 individuals. Magnification approx. x 30.

Protozoans

The animal-like **protistans** are sometimes known collectively as **protozoans.** Protozoans are found everywhere there is moisture, including ocean and freshwater environments, damp soil, and the moist interior of other **organisms.**

Protozoans are unable to make their own food, so they must find and consume it. They move actively through their environment in search of nutrition. Some are grazers, others **predators**, and some are **parasites.** Here are some examples.

Amoebalike protozoans

Amoebalike protozoans are very common everywhere in soil and water. They move around by forming pseudopods (meaning "false feet"), temporary extensions of the cell formed by **microfilaments.** Most feed by completely surrounding their prey, which can be either smaller protozoans or **algae,** and engulfing it (phagocytosis). The food item ends up enclosed inside the cell in a **vacuole,** into which digestive **enzymes** are secreted. The digested prey then passes back into the **cytoplasm,** and any undigestable material is expelled from the cell.

Foraminifera and radiolaria

Foraminifera and radiolaria have hard, protective shells through which long, threadlike pseudopodia extend. These act as sticky traps to catch other microorganisms.

Ciliophora

The ciliophora, or ciliated protozoans, have numerous tiny **cilia** on their surface. Most ciliates use these to swim through their watery environments, where they prey on bacteria, algae, and each other. The cilia beat in waves, propelling the organism along, and sweeping food particles into the cell. Ciliates are unusual in possessing two types of **nuclei.** The larger macronucleus controls the cell's **metabolism,** while the smaller micronucleus is involved only in reproduction.

The *Amoeba proteus* puts out pseudopodia to engulf another amoeba of the same species. Magnification approx. x 150.

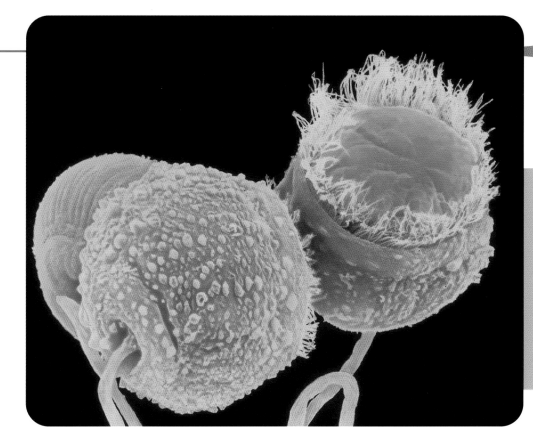

The ciliates come in a variety of shapes. *Vorticella,* for example, is a group of bell-shaped cells that attach themselves to a surface (such as the leaf of an aquatic plant) by a long, stalklike extension. *Paramecium* on the other hand is a streamlined, oval cell that is completely covered with cilia. It shoots out tiny poisonous threads called trichocysts when it is irritated.

Sporozoans

Sporozoans are parasitic protistans that complete part of their life cycle inside other cells. At one end of the cell body, there is a cluster of distinctive **organelles** used to penetrate host cells. The life cycle is often complex, involving several different host species.

Malaria: a sporozoan disease

The best-known example of a sporozoan is *Plasmodium*, which causes malaria. *Plasmodium* gets into humans through the bite of an infected female mosquito. Infective cells called sporozoites, which are similar to **spores,** are introduced into the victim's blood. These cells reproduce first in the liver and then in red blood cells. Some of the sporozoites grow and produce sex cells while in the blood, and these are picked up if the infected person is bitten again by a mosquito. Inside the mosquito's digestive tract hundreds of new sporozoite cells are formed. These travel to the mosquito's salivary glands, ready to infect the next person it bites.

4 Bacteria: The Prokaryotes

Bacteria are as diverse as any other kingdom in the natural world. One bacterium can be as distinct from another as a kangaroo is from a flea. Of all living **organisms,** bacteria are the most widespread. They are found almost everywhere on Earth, including places where other organisms could not survive. Some thrive at temperatures of 230°F (110°C) or more. Others live in acid soils and waters, in extremely salty environments, or under the high pressure and freezing conditions at the bottom of the ocean. Bacteria have been found living more than 8,205 feet (2,500 meters) below the earth's surface and in the air more than 5 miles (8 kilometers) above it. They are in soil, water droplets, and dust particles in the air and inside the digestive system of all animals. The bacteria you carry around outnumber the cells that make up your body by ten to one.

Bacterial shapes and sizes

Bacteria are grouped into three basic categories according to their shape:
- the cocci, roughly spherical in form
- the bacilli, rod-shaped, or cylindrical in form with rounded ends
- the spirilla, rigid, spiral, or coiled rods.

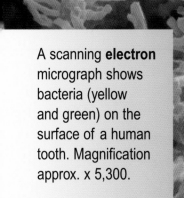

A scanning **electron** micrograph shows bacteria (yellow and green) on the surface of a human tooth. Magnification approx. x 5,300.

However, these categories are something of a simplification, as some cocci can be oval or flattened, bacilli can be long and thin like straws, and some bacteria found in salty ponds are square-shaped. Bacteria are much smaller than the cells that make up multicellular organisms such as plants and animals. The average bacterium is about a tenth the size of an average plant or animal cell.

Bacteria on the outside

Bacterial cells are usually surrounded by a protective cell wall. If fact, many types of bacteria can be identified by their cell walls. Doctors use a common laboratory test to identify which kind of bacteria is causing an infection. This helps them decide which **antibiotics** would be most effective against the infection.

Around the cell wall there may be a sticky mesh, forming a capsule or slime layer around the bacterium. This helps the bacterium to attach itself to surfaces such as rocks or teeth. The mesh also gives the bacterium an added layer of protection.

Bacteria on the inside

The **DNA** of a bacterium is contained in a single, circular **chromosome** and in smaller circular structures called **plasmids.** A bacterium has no large internal structures such as **chloroplasts** or **mitochondria.** Few bacteria have any internal divisions at all, and all the processes of their **metabolism** are carried out in the **cytoplasm** or on the **cell membrane.** However, there are **ribosomes** for **protein** production scattered throughout the cytoplasm or attached to the inside of the **plasma membrane.**

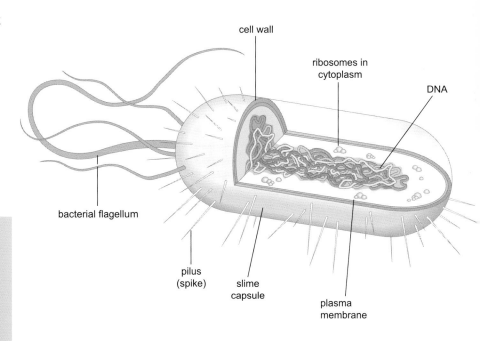

cell wall
ribosomes in cytoplasm
DNA
bacterial flagellum
pilus (spike)
slime capsule
plasma membrane

This illustration shows the structure of a typical rod-shaped bacterium.

Archaebacteria: Life at the Extreme

Until recently it was believed that life could be split neatly into two groups, or kingdoms: the **prokaryotes,** which have no **nucleus** in their cells, and the **eukaryotes**, which do. Then in 1977, Carl R. Woese of the University of Illinois discovered that a group of microorganisms that had until then been classified as bacteria were actually different enough to be given their own kingdom in the living world. This has led to a division of the prokaryotes into two distinct kingdoms: the **archaebacteria** (ancient bacteria) and the eubacteria (true bacteria).

Archaebacteria are similar to the eubacteria in many ways. They too lack a nucleus, for example. However, archaebacteria have some genes that are found in eukaryotes rather than prokaryotes. More important, more than half the genes of an archaebacterium are completely different from the genes of any other **organism.** These unshared genes may offer valuable clues to the origin and evolution of life on Earth.

Early life

Many archaebacteria and some eubacteria are adapted to the conditions widely believed to have existed on early Earth, such as great heat and little or no oxygen. For this reason most scientists suspect that the two groups developed from a common ancestor relatively soon after life began.

The gut of a cow is home to many archaebacteria.

Extremophiles

Most archaebacteria are tough creatures found in some of Earth's most extreme environments, for example near volcanic vents or in salt concentrations that would kill other organisms. For this reason they are also known as **extremophiles.**

Some of the best-known extremophiles are the deep-sea bacteria such as *Pyrococcus furiosus* (the "Flaming Fireball"). They are found near volcanic vents 9,846 feet (3,000 meters) below the ocean surface. Superheated lava oozes out of these vents at temperatures up to 752°F (400°C). Bacteria such as *Pyrococcus* are found living near these vents, at temperatures of around 212°F (100 °C).

Another group of archaebacteria, the halophiles, live in extremely salty environments, such as salt lakes and evaporation ponds where salt is collected. An ordinary cell suspended in a very salty solution quickly loses water and becomes dehydrated, because water tends to flow from areas of low salt concentration to areas of higher concentration. Halophiles deal with this problem by having high concentrations of salt within their cell. One archaean, known as *Halobacterium salinarum*, concentrates potassium chloride, a type of salt, in its interior.

Perhaps the grimmest of all the environments where extremophiles are found is hot, concentrated sulphuric acid. Some bacteria that live in hot volcanic springs, such as the geysers in Yellowstone National Park, use sulphur as a source of energy and produce sulphuric acid as a waste product. These bacteria thrive in strong sulphuric acid at 185°F (85°C).

If there is life elsewhere in the solar system, buried deep in Martian rocks or hidden beneath the ice in the oceans of Jupiter's moon Europa, it may well resemble the extremophiles.

The great Salt Lake in Utah is both very salty and alkaline (the opposite of acid). Some archaebacteria can live even in this extreme environment.

Bacterial Behavior

Many bacteria have chemical receptors that allow them to detect changes in the concentration of chemicals in their surroundings, such as sugars, oxygen, and carbon dioxide. Bacteria can also sense changes in temperature, and **photosynthetic** bacteria respond to changes in light. A few bacteria can sense the direction of a magnetic field. These bacteria have a chain of tiny particles of a magnetic material called magnetite inside their cells. This acts like a tiny compass. In water they use this ability to reach their preferred environment by swimming along magnetic lines of force.

Magnetic Martians

In the year 2000, an international team of researchers discovered long chains of magnetite crystals embedded in a meteorite that reached Earth from Mars. The magnetite crystals are similar to those formed by magnetic bacteria on Earth. Some scientists believe these chains could only have been formed by once-living **organisms.** "Such a chain of magnets outside an organism would immediately collapse into a clump due to magnetic forces," said Dr. Imre Friedmann of NASA's (National Aeronautics and Space Administration) Ames Research Center.

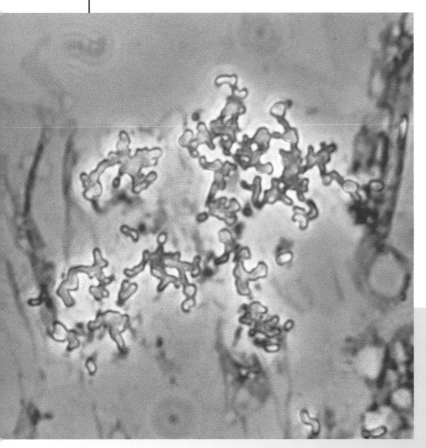

While swimming, bacteria are constantly monitoring the concentration of chemicals in their environment. The concentrations of these chemicals can affect the direction in which the bacteria move. For example, millions of *Myxococcus xanthus* bacteria will change direction to move toward a possible food source, such as other bacteria. The "prey" bacteria get stuck to the *Myxococcus* colony, which produces **enzymes** to digest them.

These bacteria (*Thiobacillus thioparvus*) need sulphur in their diet. They can sense substances containing sulphur and move toward them to feed. Magnification approx. x 800.

Getting around

Many bacteria have no means of moving themselves and simply float aimlessly in the water or are carried on the wind or on animals they have infected. Others, however, can move about by means of tiny hairlike **flagella.** These hollow, rodlike structures are formed from long strands of protein that project through the bacterium's cell wall. They are much simpler in structure than the flagella of **eukaryote** cells. The flagellum rotates like a propeller, moving the bacterium along.

Growth and reproduction

Bacterial cells live their lives at a far faster rate than eukaryote cells. Some of their enzyme systems operate very quickly indeed. Whereas it might take a cell in your body some minutes to assemble a **protein molecule,** a bacterium can do it in seconds. Under the most favorable conditions, some bacteria can reproduce and double in number every twenty minutes or so. Under natural conditions, however, limited food supplies mean that bacteria only divide every few days.

Bacterial cell division occurs by binary fission (splitting in two). The two resulting cells may separate from each other or remain attached to form a chain or filament of bacteria.

If conditions are unfavorable, some bacteria form a thick-walled structure called an endospore around their **DNA** and some of their **cytoplasm.** The endospore is resistant to heat, drying, radiation, boiling, and disinfectants. Endospores can remain dormant for many years until conditions improve. The endospore then becomes active once again, developing into a new bacterium.

A *Staphylococcus epidermidis* bacterium is shown here in the process of dividing. Under optimum conditions a single bacterium could in theory form a colony of billions within one day. Magnification approx. x 130,000.

33

Bacterial Metabolism

Bacteria are extremely small and have no internal structures, but this does not mean that they are simple. Bacteria have a wider variety of ways of obtaining energy than other types of cells do. Like other **organisms,** bacteria can be divided into self-feeders, or autotrophs (organisms such as green plants that can manufacture their food from simple raw materials), and other feeders, or heterotrophs (organisms such as humans and other animals that have to eat other organisms to get food). Autotrophs use carbon dioxide from the air as their major source of carbon, linking it with other chemicals to manufacture the materials they need. Heterotrophs consume carbon compounds that have been produced by other organisms. Most bacteria are heterotrophs.

Bacteria that eat like plants

Some autotrophic bacteria use energy from sunlight to make sugars from carbon dioxide and water, just as plants do. Many of them use a type of **chlorophyll** to capture the sun's energy. The blue-green bacteria, or cyanobacteria, make sugars in this way.

Two other groups, the green and the purple sulphur bacteria, use light energy to split compounds such as hydrogen sulphide, rather than water. No oxygen is released in this process.

Some bacteria can obtain energy from chemicals instead of from light. They use this energy to produce the food they need. This process is called **chemosynthesis** rather than **photosynthesis.**

Many of the bacteria that live around volcanic vents deep in the sea are chemosynthetic. They make food and get energy from hydrogen sulphide and other chemicals that pour out of the vents.

Salmonella are bacteria that move around using **flagella.** They live in the digestive systems of many types of mammals. Some kinds of *Salmonella* cause diseases in humans, such as salmonellosis and typhoid. Magnification approx. x 11,000.

Bacteria that eat like animals

Just like animals, most bacteria get their food already made. Bacteria feed on a wide range of materials, including both living and dead plant and animal materials. Bacteria that feed on dead materials are a vital part of the living world. They act as decomposers and recyclers, making raw materials available for reuse by the food producers. Bacteria that feed on living organisms are generally **parasites,** and often cause disease.

Bacteria break down their food by producing **enzymes** that leave the bacterium and digest the food outside the cell. The bacteria then absorbs the digested food. When a piece of food goes bad and turns mushy, it is often because it is being broken down by millions of bacteria.

Respiration

Most bacteria need oxygen for **respiration,** just as we do. But there are also some **anaerobic** bacteria. Oxygen is a poison to many of these bacteria. They obtain their energy by **fermenting** sugar. Some of these bacteria are very useful because they produce **lactic acid.** They are used in the production of butter and yogurt. Other bacteria convert alcohol into acetic acid and are used to make vinegar. Still others produce methane gas, a valuable fuel that is becoming more widespread as an energy source.

The green surface of this puddle is produced by **cyanobacteria.** Cyanobacteria are plantlike bacteria that make their own food by photosynthesis. The ancestors of today's cyanobacteria were probably the first living things on Earth to photosynthesize.

5 Viruses: Out on the Border

Viruses are simple but effective disease agents. Viruses have been found in plants, insects, mammals, fish, **protistans,** and bacteria. There are no cell types that are immune from virus attack. Viruses themselves are not complete living **organisms.** They lie on the border between the living and nonliving worlds. They are true **parasites,** entirely dependent on a living organism, called a host, for their needs.

A virus is essentially a set of instructions for making a new virus (a **DNA** or **RNA molecule** wrapped up in a protective coat). The virus cannot read these instructions by itself. Viruses lack the **enzymes** and other chemicals necessary for reproduction. The only way they can reproduce is by entering a living cell and taking over its biochemical processes. The damage caused to cells by the assembly of the new viruses produces the symptoms of viral disease.

There may only be enough genetic material in a small virus for three or four genes, while larger viruses will have around 100 genes. Compare this to the 30,000 or so genes in humans.

Viruses range in size from 0.78 to 7.8 millionths of an inch (20 to 200 millionths of a millimeter). The period at the end of this sentence is around 0.02 inch (.5 millimeter) across—big enough to hold about 5,000 medium-sized viruses.

Although the existence of viruses was suspected by the end of the nineteenth century, it was not until the **electron microscope** was perfected in the years after World War II that scientists first saw what a virus looked like. Viruses come in a variety of shapes and cause a wide variety of diseases. AIDS, rabies, polio, measles, influenza, and the common cold are just a few examples of viral diseases.

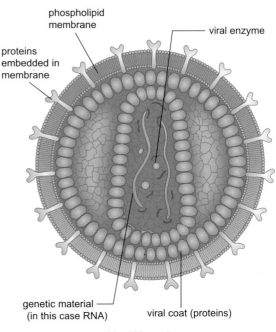

phospholipid membrane

viral enzyme

proteins embedded in membrane

genetic material (in this case RNA)

viral coat (proteins)

100—120 nm diameter

Simple viruses consist of a strand of either DNA or RNA surrounded by a coat of protein, or protein and **lipid.** Some viruses are more complex, with a membrane around the DNA or RNA and perhaps tail fibers and other structures.

Mounting a defense

The human body has several lines of defense against viral attacks. First, if a particular virus infects some of the cells in your body, the infected cells make a type of **protein** called interferon. Interferon works with the cells surrounding the infected cells, helping them to become more resistant to the virus. Sometimes this works, but sometimes it doesn't. If the resistance is not strong enough, the virus continues to spread and affect more and more cells.

Another line of defense is the body's immune system. It acts by killing infected cells. Killing infected cells is similar to making a firebreak to keep a forest fire from spreading. A virus needs a living cell in order to reproduce itself. By killing infected cells, the immune system takes away the virus's fuel. Eventually, if the immune system does its job, the virus will run out of places to make new viruses.

Antibodies are the body's most effective defense against viruses. Antibodies are proteins produced by the immune system. They bind with the virus, making it harmless or destroying it altogether. The body makes large amounts of antibodies when a virus is detected. However, antibodies have no effect against viruses that are already inside cells.

Where did they come from?

No one knows how viruses originally came about. They may have originated as pieces of genetic material that escaped from cells and gained the ability to reproduce themselves by passing from one cell to another.

Bacteriophages are complex viruses that infect bacteria. The T4 bacteriophage shown here attaches to the outside of a bacterium and injects its DNA into the cell. Magnification approx. x 150,000.

6 Under the Microscope

Cells are too small to be seen with the naked eye. Until the invention of the **microscope,** no one had any idea that cells existed at all.

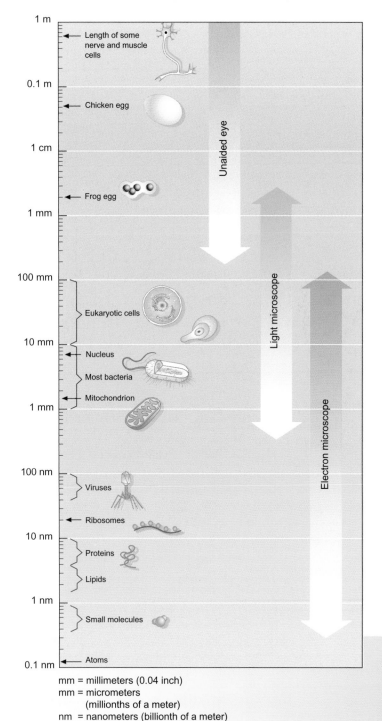

- 1 m — Length of some nerve and muscle cells
- 0.1 m — Chicken egg
- 1 cm
- Frog egg
- 1 mm
- 100 mm — Eukaryotic cells
- 10 mm — Nucleus / Most bacteria
- 1 mm — Mitochondrion
- 100 nm — Viruses
- Ribosomes
- 10 nm — Proteins / Lipids
- 1 nm — Small molecules
- 0.1 nm — Atoms

Unaided eye
Light microscope
Electron microscope

mm = millimeters (0.04 inch)
mm = micrometers (millionths of a meter)
nm = nanometers (billionth of a meter)

The compound microscope

In a modern compound light microscope, two or more lenses bend light reflected from the object being examined to form an enlarged image of it. Compound microscopes are widely used in biology and medicine to study bacteria and other single-celled **organisms** and plant and animal cells. Compound microscopes have a maximum magnification of about 1,000 to 1,500 times. They can show structures in the cell such as the **nucleus, chloroplasts,** and **mitochondria.**

Biologists use a variety of techniques when studying cells with a compound microscope. They can take very thin sections of cells with an instrument called a microtome and use dyes to pick out various cell structures. Digital video microscopy makes use of advances in digital video cameras and computer enhancement to observe living cells. Using this technique, biologists can study small, transparent objects that would otherwise be almost impossible to see.

The naked eye can distinguish objects about 0.02 inch (0.5 millimeter) apart. A light microscope can separate objects less than 1/25,400 inch (1 micrometer) apart, but an electron microscope can distinguish objects down to almost 0.1 nanometer (billionth of a meter).

The electron microscope

Instead of lenses and light rays, the **electron microscope** uses electromagnetic fields to focus a stream of subatomic particles called **electrons** onto an object. The image appears on a fluorescent screen, similar to a television. An electron microscope can give 100 times greater magnification than a light microscope. It reveals more of the detailed structure of the cell.

There are two basic types of electron microscopes. The transmission electron microscope projects a beam of electrons through the specimen being observed. Samples to be studied using a transmission electron microscope must be very thin.

The scanning electron microscope sends a narrow beam of electrons back and forth across a specimen that has had a very thin coat of metal applied to it. The metal gives off electrons, which are picked up by a detector to produce an image of the specimen on a television screen. The scanning electron microscope produces images of fantastic depth and clarity.

The electron microscope allows scientists to examine the detailed structure of **organelles** such as the mitochondria and reveals structures such as **ribosomes,** which are too small to be seen with a light microscope. Scientists can also see **viruses,** which are smaller than the smallest bacterium.

Van Leeuwenhoek

In the last half of the 1600s, a Dutch businessman named Antonie van Leeuwenhoek made hand-polished lenses that could magnify an incredible 300 times. With his simple, single-lens microscopes he became the first person to observe living cells, including blood cells and single-celled organisms in pond water. His lenses were so good that he might have been the first person to see bacteria.

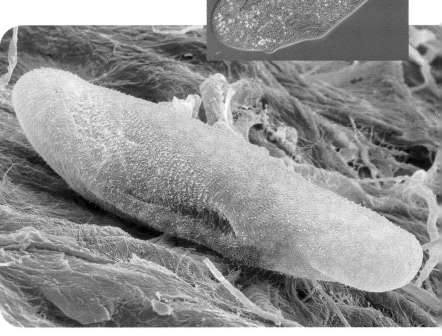

These are two images of the **protistan** *Paramecium*. The top picture is from a light microscope. The lower one is from a scanning electron microscope. The light microscope image shows details from inside the cell, but it's two-dimensional. Magnifications x 640 (top) and x 800 (below).

7 First Cells

Cells are made of a complex soup of chemicals, all reacting together in a controlled way to produce what we call life. Cells assemble all the **molecules** they need, such as **proteins, carbohydrates,** and **nucleic acids,** using simpler compounds and energy that they obtain from their environment. The result of all this complex chemical interaction is movement, feeding, reproduction, and all the other characteristics of life. But how did this all come about?

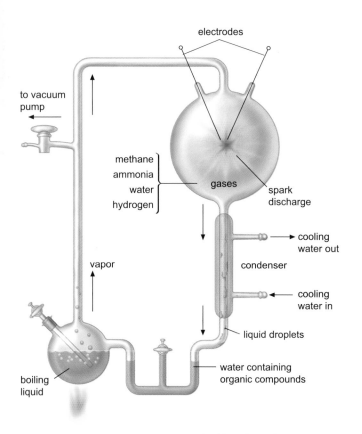

This diagram shows the apparatus Miller and Urey used to simulate the conditions in which we think early life arose.

As far as we know, Earth spent the first 500 million years of its existence being hit by huge meteorites, which were pieces of rock left over from the formation of the solar system. Some of these collisions were so ferocious that the oceans boiled and turned to gas. At least one impact was powerful enough to knock off a chunk of Earth (this chunk became the moon). The young sun was weaker than it is now and even after the worst of the bombardment was over, Earth was gripped by planetwide ice ages.

Despite the harshness of the conditions, somehow, probably during the first billion years of Earth's history, complex molecules began forming and reproducing themselves. They got their energy from chemicals or sunlight. All the chemicals needed to form organic molecules were present on early Earth and perhaps lightning, energy from the sun, or heat from inside Earth provided the energy to form more complex molecules.

Life modeling

In 1953 Harold Urey and Stanley Miller carried out an experiment to show that it was possible to produce organic molecules under conditions believed to resemble those found on Earth billions of years ago. They mixed methane, hydrogen, ammonia, and water inside a reaction chamber and then bombarded the mixture with electrical discharges to simulate lightning. In less than a week, **amino acids** and other organic compounds had formed.

Shaping life from clay?

Urey and Miller's experiment showed that it was possible to form simple organic compounds. But how did more complex molecules form? One theory is that flat beds of clay, washed by the tides, were sites for the assembly of proteins and other compounds. Clay is made up of thin layers of material with ions (charged particles) that attract amino acids at their surfaces. If you expose amino acids to clay, warm the clay in the sun, and alternately moisten and dry it (as would happen with the rise and fall of the tides), reactions take place that produce proteins and other compounds.

Giant tubeworms and tiny white crabs are among the creatures that thrive around vents, such as this hydrothermal vent in the Pacific Ocean.

Another theory is that organic compounds formed near hydrothermal vents—places where hot volcanic lava bursts out from inside the Earth onto the ocean floor. These are the sort of places where **archaebacteria** are found today. Experiments have shown that when amino acids are heated and placed in water, they form small proteinlike molecules called proteinoids.

Chemical competition

If some of the proteins formed by whatever means acted as **enzymes,** promoting the formation of other proteins, an evolutionary "protein competition" could have begun. The next step might have been the emergence of **metabolism**, the harnessing of energy to bring about chemical reactions. Metabolism is a key characteristic of life.

If organic compounds such as enzymes and **ATP** formed in the same location, they would begin to react together chemically and so, over time, the pattern of reactions found in cell metabolism today could begin to emerge.

Another characteristic of living things is their ability to reproduce. To do this they must make copies of **DNA** molecules. How DNA first emerged, we do not yet know.

Building Cells

The proteinoids mentioned earlier were found to form small stable spheres after cooling. Could a similar process have led to the formation of the first **cell membranes?** Like cell membranes, proteinoid spheres are selectively permeable, allowing some substances in and out but not others. Other experiments have produced membranelike sacs from **lipids** (fats). Such spheres that form around **proteins, ATP,** and other chemicals would protect and isolate them from the environment, perhaps allowing the development of **metabolic** processes.

Earliest life

The first identifiable living cells appeared perhaps 3.9 billion years ago. How and where this happened, we will never know. We believe that they were similar to today's bacteria. In other words, they were **prokaryote** cells lacking a **nucleus.** Possibly they were not much different from the lipid spheres described above. They had plenty of time to develop. Food was abundant, energy plentiful, and there were no **predators.**

These protein and lipid spheres were created in the laboratory. They have the same properties as the cell membranes found in living **organisms.** Magnification approx. x 400.

At some point the family line diverged. One branch became the eubacteria and the other gave rise to the **archaebacteria** and eventually the **eukaryotes,** which would one day lead to the huge variety of multicellular life that includes humans.

Between 3.5 and 3.2 billion years ago, the first photosynthesizers appeared. This was a major step in the development of life. **Photosynthesis** not only made the vast source of energy from the sun available to Earth's developing life forms, it also released oxygen into the atmosphere. This had a profound effect. Oxygen is a very active chemical and prevents complex organic compounds from forming. So the cells that populated Earth at that time had to adapt to the new oxygen-rich atmosphere, or live in places where oxygen was scarce.

Another consequence of the rising oxygen levels was that the conditions under which life originally emerged were now gone for good. Life would not be able to start from scratch again, because the delicate molecules involved would be disrupted by the reactive oxygen.

Endosymbiosis

Eukaryotic cells, the kind that make up the human body, may have come about by a series of happy accidents. According to one theory, eukaryotes appeared as a result of endosymbiosis. *Endo-* means "within," and *symbiosis* means "living together." Around 1.2 billion years ago, the ancestors of the eukaryotes may have been something like amoebae that engulfed aerobic bacteria. Perhaps some of these bacteria resisted being digested and began to live inside larger cells, benefiting from the protection this gave them. Eventually these bacterial cells became the **mitochondria** that all eukaryote cells now contain. **Chloroplasts** may have arisen in a similar way.

Once the first eukaryotes appeared, the stage was set for the next great evolutionary step: the emergence of multicellular life.

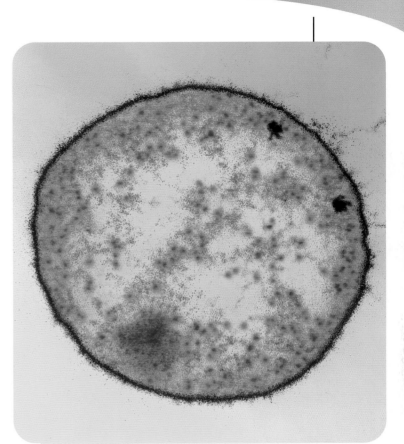

Early forms of life may have looked similar to simple bacteria such as this archaebacterium *Methanococcoides burtonii*. Magnification approx. x 120,000.

Out of this world cells?

In an experiment that duplicated the harsh conditions of space, including very cold temperatures, no air, and a lot of radiation, scientists managed to get artificial cell membranes to form. The researchers used simple, common compounds, which self-assembled into something that looked a lot like a cell membrane. These compounds have been found on dust from meteorites carried to Earth, and years ago they were found to form soapy, water-repelling bubbles. Scientists believe the **molecules** needed to make a cell membrane can be found throughout space.

The researchers suggest that organic compounds from interstellar space might have kick-started life on Earth. The scientists are trying to make a model of what might have led to early life by placing **nucleic acids** inside their artificial membranes and feeding them with chemicals known to support cell activity.

The Chemistry of Life—A Summary

The keys to life are the following:

1. All life consists of one or more cells.

2. All life is made from the same materials.

3. All life must acquire energy and raw materials to use for growth, to maintain itself, and to reproduce. This process is called **metabolism.**

4. All life can react to changes in its external and internal environments.

5. Instructions for **protein** production coded in DNA control the development of multicellular organisms and give all life the ability to grow and reproduce.

Carbohydrates, **lipids**, proteins, and **nucleic acids** are the basic ingredients of all cells—the materials that life is built on. All are complex organic compounds called macromolecules, large molecules made up of many smaller repeating units.

Carbohydrates

Carbohydrates contain only the elements carbon, hydrogen, and oxygen.

Simple sugars
These usually have four to six carbons and are used by the cell as an energy source. **Glucose** is the most common sugar in all cells. Fructose is an important sugar in plant cells. Sucrose, or table sugar, is glucose and fructose joined together.

Polysaccharides
These are macromolecules that are made up of many simple sugar units. For example, **starch** is used as an energy store in plants, while plant cell walls are made of **cellulose.** Glycogen is an energy-storing **molecule** found in animals.

Proteins

Proteins are used as structural materials, for cell movement, for defense against disease, and most important, for controlling the rates of chemical reactions in cells.

Proteins are made up of long chains of smaller molecules called **amino acids.** Amino acids contain carbon, hydrogen, oxygen, and an extra element, nitrogen. Some amino acids also contain sulphur.

Fibrous proteins
These are proteins that form long strands or sheets. Examples are keratin, found in hair and nails, and collagen, found in bone.

Globular proteins
In these proteins the long molecules fold up to make complex three-dimensional shapes. **Enzymes** are globular proteins. Another example is hemoglobin, the protein that carries oxygen in red blood cells.

Lipids

Lipids are molecules that contain few oxygen **atoms** and many hydrogen and carbon atoms. They do not dissolve readily in water.

Fats and oils
Fats and oils are used for energy storage. The fats found in butter and olive oil are examples of this type of lipid.

Phospholipids
These are lipids that contain the element phosphorus. They are the main structural material of **cell membranes.**

Waxes
Waxes are waterproofing materials used to cover leaves and other plant parts above the ground.

Cholesterol
One of a group of lipids that are a major part of animal cell membranes.

Nucleic acids

Nucleic acids are formed from chains of smaller molecules called nucleotides. Nucleotides, like amino acids, contain nitrogen. **ATP** is a nucleotide.

DNA
DNA is made up of two linked chains of nucleotides twisted in a double spiral. The instructions for making proteins are encoded in the structure of the DNA molecule.

RNA
Single-chain molecules similar to DNA but with slightly different nucleotides. One type, **messenger RNA (mRNA),** is formed by transcription of DNA. This mRNA is then translated by RNA and **ribosomes** into amino acid chains, which then become proteins.

Glossary

adenosine triphosphate (ATP) energy-carrying molecule that powers most of the activity in both plant and animal cells

aerobic respiration *see respiration*

algae large group of plantlike protistans, mostly living in water. They range from microscopic single-celled organisms to giant kelp seaweeds.

amino acid naturally occurring chemical used by cells to make proteins

anaerobic respiration *see respiration*

antibiotic chemical that can destroy or stop the growth of disease-causing bacteria and other microorganisms

archaebacterium group of bacteria that are very different from other bacterial groups (the eubacteria)

ATP *see adenosine triphosphate*

carbohydrate chemical compound composed of carbon, hydrogen, and oxygen. Glucose is a simple carbohydrate.

carotenoid one of a group of pigments found in plants. Carotenoids give the red color to autumn leaves.

cell membrane outer boundary of a cell, made of a double layer of lipid and protein molecules

cellulose type of complex carbohydrate that forms the cell wall of plant cells

chemosynthesis process in which living things make their own food using chemicals to provide the energy needed. Some bacteria are chemosynthetic.

chlorophyll light-capturing pigment found in plant cells that is involved in photosynthesis. Chlorophyll gives plants their green color.

chloroplast structure found inside plant cells where photosynthesis takes place

chromosome a threadlike structure that becomes visible in a cell's nucleus just before it divides. Chromosomes contain a cell's genetic material (DNA).

cilium (plural cilia) thin, hairlike structures that project in large numbers from some cells. They are used for movement.

crista (plural cristae) folds inside a mitochondrion where some of the enzymes involved in respiration are found

cytomembrane system system of membranes and structures inside a cell that package and distribute newly formed proteins

cytoplasm all of the parts of a cell between the nucleus and the cell membrane

cytoskeleton internal framework of microtubules and other components that supports the cell and moves its organelles around

cytosol fluid or jellylike part of the cytoplasm that surrounds all the organelles in eukaryote cells

deoxyribonucleic acid (DNA) genetic material found in all cells, by which a living thing passes on its characteristics to the next generation. DNA carries coded instructions for building the cell's many proteins.

diffusion process by which molecules move from one place to another

DNA *see deoxyribonucleic acid*

electron tiny particle within an atom. Electrons form the outside of an atom, orbiting around a central nucleus.

electron microscope *see microscope*

endocytosis process by which a cell takes in a substance by folding the cell membrane around it

endoplasmic reticulum (ER) a network of membranes that runs through the cytoplasm of eukaryote cells. Parts of the rough endoplasmic reticulum are covered with ribosomes, which are where proteins are manufactured.

enzyme protein molecule that greatly speeds up a reaction in a cell, or enables the reaction to happen

eukaryote cell that contains a nucleus and other organelles. All cells, with the exception of bacteria, are eukaryote cells.

extremophile bacterium that lives in an extreme environment, for instance at a high temperature or in very acidic conditions

fermentation type of anaerobic respiration which is a means of generating energy from glucose without the use of oxygen

flagellum (plural flagella) long, whiplike structure found projecting from the surface of some cells. Flagella are used for movement.

glucose simple carbohydrate made by plants during photosynthesis and used by all living things as a source of energy in respiration

glycolysis first part of the energy-releasing process in a cell (respiration). A series of reactions in which glucose is broken down into two simpler compounds and energy is released.

Golgi body structure inside a cell responsible for packaging proteins and other substances that are manufactured inside the cell and are ready for export

Krebs cycle part of the chemical process in cells for releasing energy from glucose, fats, and proteins

lactic acid waste product of one form of anaerobic respiration

lipid greasy or oily substance produced by cells for making cell membranes and for other purposes. Fats are lipids.

lysosome small membrane-bound structures within cells that contain powerful digestive enzymes. They are used to destroy worn-out organelles or to digest food particles.

messenger RNA (mRNA) *see ribonucleic acid*

metabolism total of all the chemical reactions in a cell

microfilament thin fiber attached to the cell membrane, which helps give the cell shape

microscope instrument used to make magnified images of small objects. An electron microscope is much more powerful than an optical, or light microscope. It "sees" objects using beams of electrons instead of light rays.

microtubule protein tube used by the cell to move things around. Microtubules are part of the cytoskeleton.

mitochondrion (plural mitochondria) the structure within the cell where aerobic respiration takes place. Mitochondria produce most of a cell's energy.

molecules particles made up of two or more atoms joined together

nucleic acid class of very large molecules found in living cells that includes DNA and RNA

nucleolus part of the nucleus where segments of chromosomes are unwound so their DNA can be read in order to make messenger RNA

nucleus (plural nuclei) large, membrane-bound structure in the center of a eukaryote cell where its genetic material is held

organelle structure within cells, often bound by a membrane, that carries out a specific task or tasks

organism any kind of living thing

osmosis movement of water across a partially permeable membrane (such as a cell membrane) from a less concentrated solution to a more concentrated one

parasite organism that lives on or in another organism and gets food from it without giving anything in return

photosynthesis process by which green plants and some other organisms use the energy of sunlight to make sugars (food) from carbon dioxide and water

phytoplankton single-celled, water-dwelling organisms that are capable of photosynthesis

plasma membrane another term for cell membrane

plasmid piece of DNA, usually circular, found inside a bacterium

predator organism that catches and eats other organisms for food. The organisms that a predator eats are called its prey.

prokaryote type of cell that does not have its genetic material in a nucleus. All bacteria are prokaryotes.

proteins complex organic molecules that perform a variety of essential tasks in cells, such as providing structure and acting as enzymes in chemical reactions

protistan diverse grouping of organisms. Most organisms in this group are microscopic and single-celled

protozoan protistan that is similar to an animal in that it cannot make its own food but has to "eat"

respiration the breaking down of complex molecules in living cells to release energy. This is the main way by which cells get their energy. Aerobic respiration requires oxygen, while anaerobic respiration, a less efficient process, does not.

ribonucleic acid (RNA) nucleic acid, similar to DNA, that is involved in the manufacture of proteins. Messenger RNA is made from DNA in the nucleus and acts as a template for making proteins.

ribosome structure in the cell where amino acids are put together to make proteins

spore extremely small reproductive body produced by fungi and some other living things

starch complex carbohydrate, used as a food store in plants

vacuole fluid-filled cavity inside a cell that is surrounded by a membrane

vesicle tiny membrane sac used, for example, in transporting proteins within a cell

virus nonliving agent composed of DNA or RNA with an outer protein layer that is capable of infecting a cell and using its machinery to make copies of itself

Further Reading

Wallace, Holly. *Life Processes: Cells and Systems.* Chicago: Heinemann Library, 2001.

Wallace, Holly. *Life Processes: Classification.* Chicago: Heinemann Library, 2001.

Microlife: four books about the world of microorganisms
Snedden, Robert. *A World of Microorganisms.* Chicago: Heinemann Library, 2001.
Snedden, Robert. *Scientists and Discoveries.* Chicago: Heinemann Library, 2001.
Snedden, Robert. *The Benefits of Bacteria.* Chicago: Heinemann Library, 2001.
Snedden, Robert. *Fighting Infectious Disease.* Chicago: Heinemann Library, 2001.

Index

SUGAR GROVE PUBLIC LIBRARY DISTRICT
54 Snow Street/P.O. Box 1049
Sugar Grove, IL 60554
(630) 466-4686